Daisy Goes Flying

A CO-PILOT POOCH

written by
Megan Haley

illustrated by
Sadia Atiq

Daisy was excited because she was off to fly!
She and Jeff, her human, were heading for the sky.

"It's going to be awesome!" Daisy
    thought. "A super day!"
She dragged poor Jeff out of the door...
    then they were on their way.

The day was full of fun-filled
flights, all waiting to be flown.
Jeff loved to have Daisy there,
so he was not alone.

The first flight took them up a
mountain where people could ski.
The view was something special –
snow, as far as they could see.

One skier was *SO* nervous
about taking the flight,
But he sat right next to Daisy,
who made him feel alright.

When they landed at the lodge,
the skiers jumped right out.

"Four days' skiing! WHOOP-DE-DOOOOO!" Daisy heard one shout.

Then off they went, back to the hangar. Lots to see and do. They loaded up supplies and food, all ready for flight two.

They couldn't fly just yet, though,
for they were short on fuel.
"Always fill your tank up," Jeff said.
"That's the golden rule."

So once the tank was filled right up,
back to the lodge they flew.
Jeff and Daisy made a great
supply delivery crew!

Flight number three! They picked
up the important 'Ski Patrol'.
They had to check the mountain
out for avalanche control.

When they rose above the peak,
the Ski Patrol saw trouble.
"Too much snow!" the lead called out.
"Let's clear it... on the double!"

Too much snow meant it was
    deep - too deep to ski on top.
If a skier landed hard, into the
    depths they'd 'PLOP'!

They had a special package that
would *BLAST* away the snow!
The team tossed out the heavy
bundle to the peak below.

'KABOOM!
KABLAAM!'

The package went.

'KAPOW!
KAPLOOF!
KABLARE!'

The snow was thrown from side
to side, and high into the air.

The snow began to slide away

in one GIGANTIC wave!

It seemed a little frightening,
but Daisy was so brave.

Now the slope was clear and safe,
they flew the Patrollers back.
Before they packed up for the
day, they had a little snack.

Their tasks complete, their job well done, they went home for the night. Well... they would have done had there not been *yet another* flight!

EMERGENCY!

Their help was needed fast!

Some poor young man was stuck in snow - at night, he would not last.

The man had fallen off a ledge
and badly hurt his arm.
They lifted him into a seat, and
Daisy kept him calm.

The injured man, he groaned, as they moved in to forward flight. "Don't worry, sir," said Jeff. "I'm sure that you will be alright."

A busy day! Four flights in all.
"I'm tired out," Jeff said.

"Come on Daisy, let's go home,
and snuggle up in bed."

Once they were home, they both relaxed.
They cuddled, ate, and played.
"What fun our flights were," Jeff said.
"What a difference we made!"

The night was dark. Her eyes were heavy. It was time to sleep. Daisy laid her head to rest and started counting sheep.

She drifted off in seconds, only dreams behind her eyes. Nothing but thoughts of helicopters soaring through the skies.

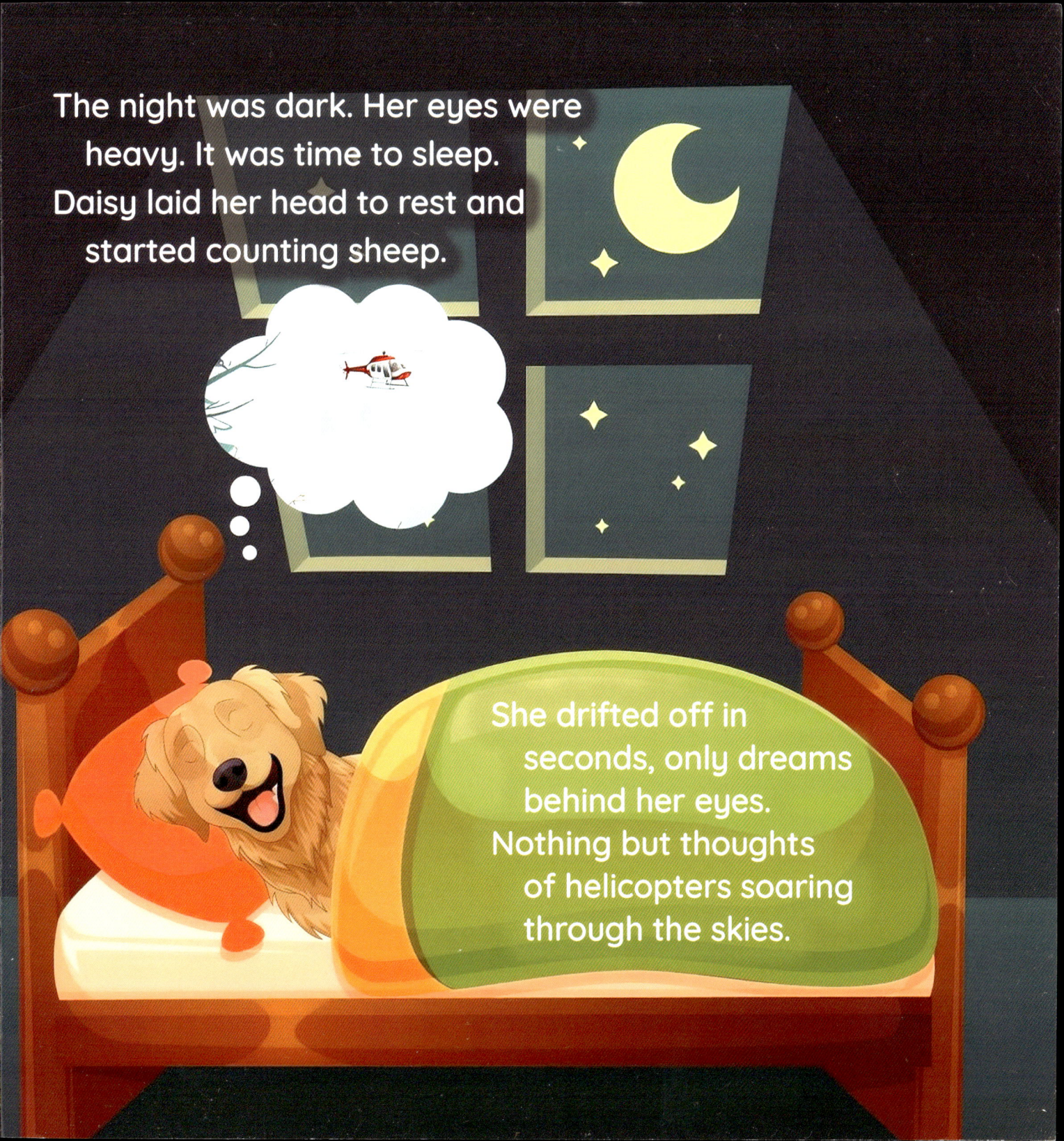

For Wyatt, Wynter & Jeff

And a huge could not have done it without you thank-yous to my mom Barb

Illustrations completed by Sadia Atiq

1st edition in Paperback 2024
ISBN: 978-1-0690927-0-0
Printed in Canada

Published by Megan Haley with assistance from Linda Gosnell